This World Of Ours Is Never Short Of Lots Of People Of Every Sort . . . .

People hot

and

People cold.....

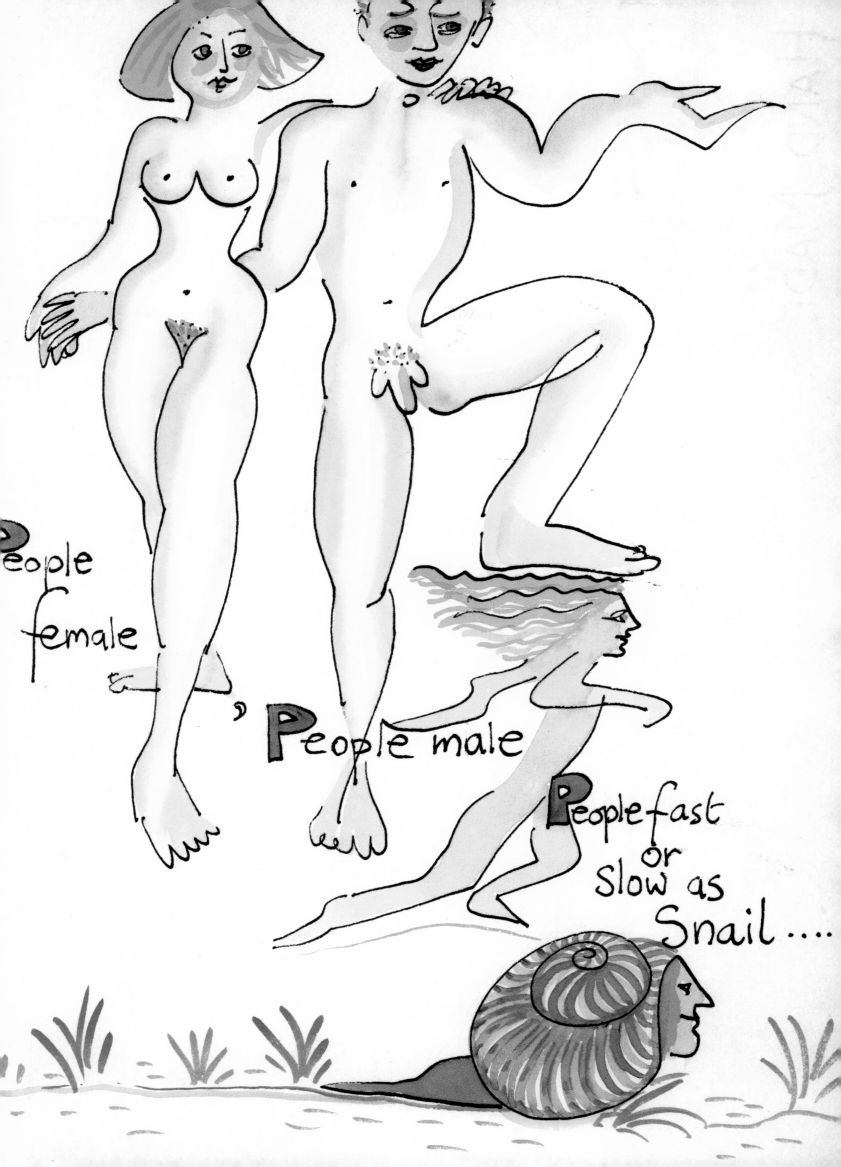

People
female

'People male

Peoplefast
or
Slow as
Snail....

People juggling bits of tin,

People who can weave and spin,

People Sharp and People mellow,
People pink and People yellow

People looking front and back,

People Red and People black, ...

People swimming,

People flying,

People laughing,

People crying,

People digging big, big holes

People

eating buttered rolls, ...

People working
farms for
food,

People being very rude

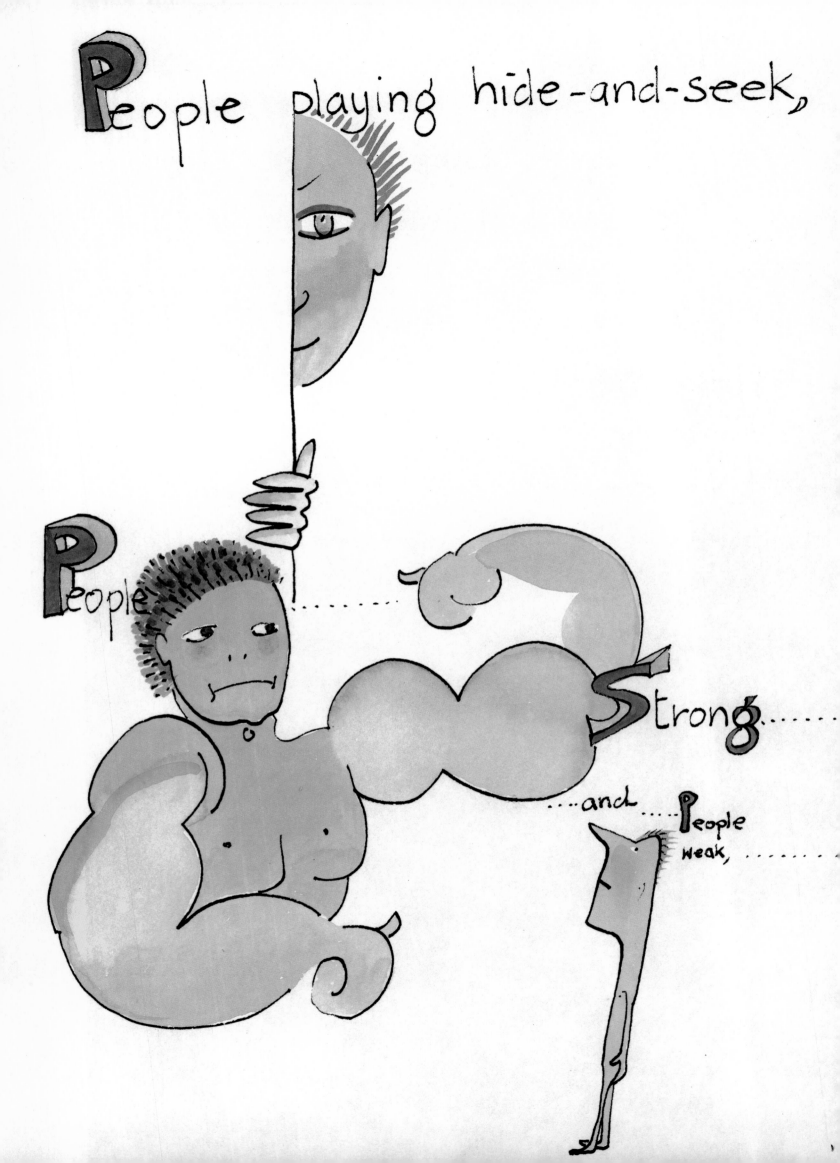

People very, very TALL,

People hardly there at all,.......

People whose friends are Oh! so MANY!

People who have hardly any,

People making brilliant guesses,
People
making AWFUL messes, ...

People counting sleeping bats,

People wearing silly HATS

People hiding secret things,

People

Watching seagull's wings

People mending broken cars,

People looking at the stars,...

People eating birthday-cake,

People weeping at a wake, ...

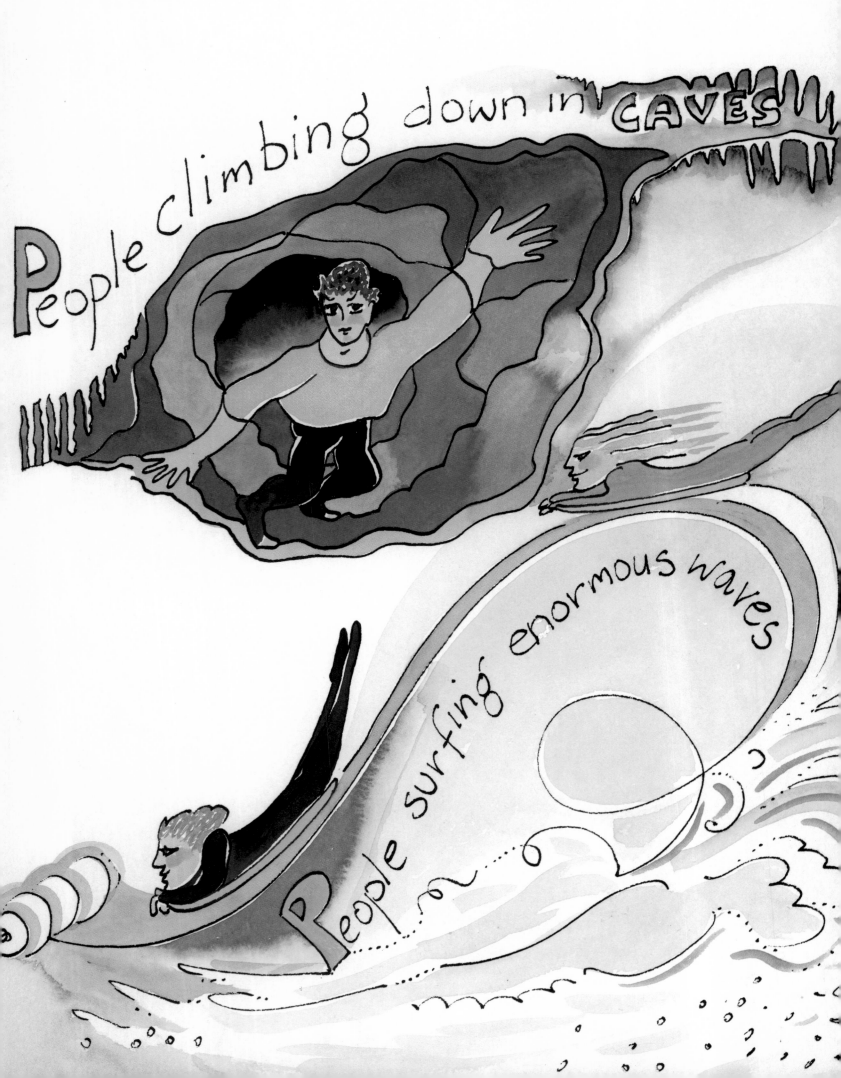

People telling bedtime stories,

People talking of past glories

People eating chinese meals.

People dancing Irish REELS.

I've tried hard, and that's my score; **I** Wonder can you think of More

and more ?
and more ?

Yes, if you look, you'll always find— more **P**eople of a different Kind...

For Sarah Emmeline and Úna Benvan
JM

To Poppy and Holly, who will be reading this book to their
offspring, and so on, and on, and on ...
PB

John Maguire, former professor of Sociology at University College
Cork, is a singer-songwriter who writes and lectures about power,
politics and peace issues. He has had songs recorded by himself and
others, and published children's poems and stories.

Pauline Bewick is one of Ireland's best known artists, renowned for
her quirky watercolours. Despite dyslexia and no formal education,
she has had a distinguished career as an artist and writer.

Published in 2001 by
The Collins Press
West Link Park
Doughcloyne
Wilton
Cork

British Library Cataloguing in Publication data.

Typesetting by Artmark

Printed by Estudios Gráficos Zure, S.A. – Bilbao (Spain)

ISBN: 1-903464-06-4